DATE DUE

Junior Science
hot and cold

Terry Jennings

Illustrations by David Anstey

Gloucester Press
New York · London · Toronto · Sydney

About this book

You can learn many different things about temperature in this book. There are many activities and experiments for you to try. You will find out what a thermometer is used for and how to take the temperature of something. You can also find out what happens when solids are heated and how some materials let heat through quickly and others slowly.

First published in the United States in 1989 by Gloucester Press 387 Park Avenue South New York, NY 10016

ISBN 0 531 17127 2

Library of Congress Catalog Card Number: 88-83099

© BLA Publishing Limited 1988

This book was designed and produced by BLA Publishing Limited, TR House, Christopher Road, East Grinstead, Sussex, England. A member of the Ling Kee Group London Hong Kong Taipei Singapore New York

Printed in Spain by Heraclio Fournier, S.A.

Look at the pictures. One of them shows hot weather and the other shows cold weather. In both of these pictures there are hot and cold objects. In the hot weather picture the ice cream is cold. In the cold weather picture the bonfire is hot.

Look around your home and try to guess which things feel warm and which things feel cold. Now touch lots of things. But do not touch things that are burning or that are very hot.

In the picture the dog, the cup of cocoa, the soup and the hot water bottle feel warm. The other things feel cold.

refrigerator

cocoa

ice

dog

hot water bottle

can of drink

bowl of soup

Our skin tells us if something is hot or cold. But sometimes our skin can be wrong. Take three bowls of water – one with very warm water, one with ice cold water and the other with lukewarm water.

Put one hand in the warm water and the other in the cold water. Then put both hands in the lukewarm water. The hand that has been in the cold water will feel hot, and the hand that has been in the warm water will feel cold.

The picture shows a thermometer. It is used to show the temperature of the room. The temperature shows how hot or cold something is. The temperature is shown in degrees Fahrenheit and Celsius. We write it as °F or °C. Water usually freezes at 32°F. Water usually boils at 212°F. This thermometer shows it is 70°F.

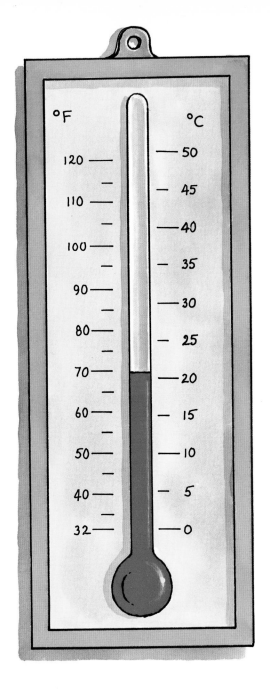

6

You can take the temperature of lots of things. Make a chart like this and see where you find the highest temperature and where you find the lowest temperature.

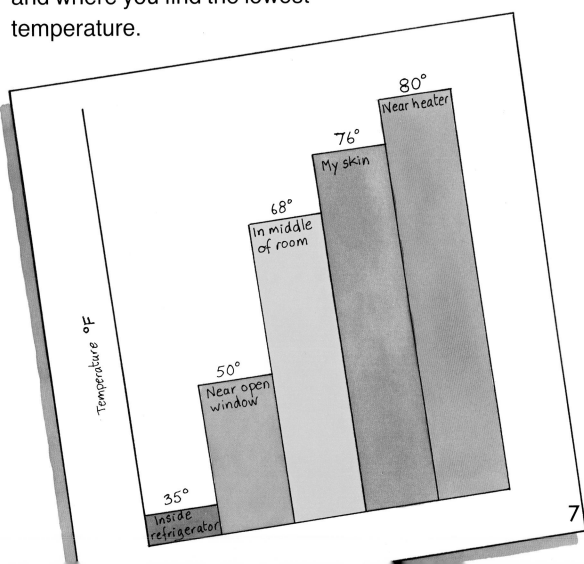

Temperature °F

80°
Near heater

76°
My skin

68°
In middle
of room

50°
Near open
window

35°
Inside
refrigerator

8

Our body temperature usually stays the same. This temperature is about 98.6°F. When you run you soon feel hot. But the temperature inside you is still 98.6°F. In cold weather you may feel cold. But the temperature inside you is still 98.6°F.

The doctor uses a special thermometer. It takes your temperature inside your mouth or under your arm. If you don't feel well your temperature may be higher than 98.6°F. The doctor may take your temperature to see if you are ill.

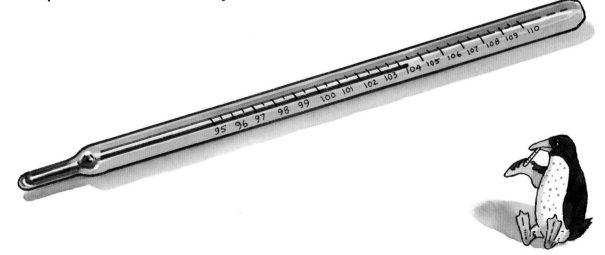

In the picture it is a lovely sunny day. But the boy does not feel warm. If he moved out from under the shade of the tree he would feel the warmth from the sun.

10

This girl has been throwing snowballs and her hands are very cold. If she rubbed her hands together very hard they would feel warmer. She could also make them warm by wearing gloves or by warming them over a radiator.

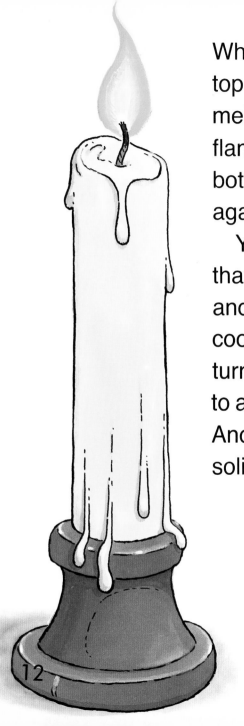

When a candle is lit the wax at the top melts. It turns into a liquid. It melts because of the heat from the flame. When the wax reaches the bottom of the candle it goes hard again. It turns solid when it cools.

You may know of other solids that melt when they are warmed and get hard again when they are cooled. In fact, all solids melt and turn into a liquid if they are heated to a high enough temperature. And they will turn back to a solid again if they are cooled.

The girl in the picture is having hamburgers, french fries and peas. They have all been cooked. This is what her lunch looked like before it was cooked.

The lunch would not be nice to eat if it wasn't cooked. If it got cold it would not go back to being the same as it was before it was cooked.

13

Some materials let heat pass through them quickly. Other materials let heat pass through them very slowly. Ask a grown-up to fill a hot water bottle for you and put it on a table. Then lay a piece of wood on top of the bottle. Put your hand on the wood and count up to 30. The wood will feel cool. It lets heat through slowly.

wood

plastic tray

metal baking tray

lid

newspaper

china plate

Now do the same thing with a metal tray. The tray
will feel hot. It lets heat through quickly. In the picture
the metal tray and the can lid let heat through
quickly and the other objects let heat through slowly.

15

This saucepan is mostly made of metal, but the handle and knob are plastic. The metal part of the pan needs to let heat pass through it quickly to heat the water inside. The handle and knob must allow heat to pass through them slowly or they will burn the user.

Draw two pictures, one of a girl and one of a boy. Cut out some pictures of clothing from an old magazine. Dress one of the children in clothing for cold weather and the other in clothing for hot weather.

Draw faces on two circles of paper and stick the faces on two empty soda cans. Wrap a piece of woollen cloth around one of the cans. Now ask a grown-up to fill both cans with hot water and put a thermometer in each can.

Pretend the cans are people and take their temperatures every five minutes for 30 minutes. Both of the cans will begin to cool, but the can without the woollen material around it will cool the fastest.

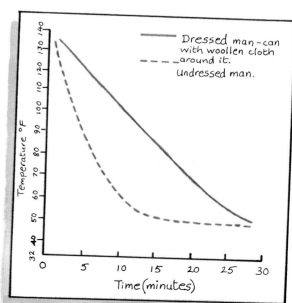

Dressed man – can with woollen cloth around it.
Undressed man.

Temperature °F

Time (minutes)

We wear clothing to keep us warm. We have blankets or quilts on our beds to keep us warm. Clothing, blankets and quilts let heat pass through them very slowly. That is the way they keep us warm. We have other ways of keeping warm in cold weather. Some people have a fire to keep their house warm.

Some people have a boiler and radiators. How is your house kept warm?

Take four ice cubes that are the same size and see which is the fastest way to melt them. Put one in a bowl of hot water, leave one out in the sun, breathe on another and rub the other in your warm hands. The ice cube in the hot water will probably melt first.

You could make the ice cubes last a long time by wrapping them in cloth or paper.

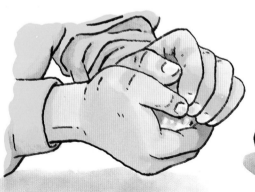

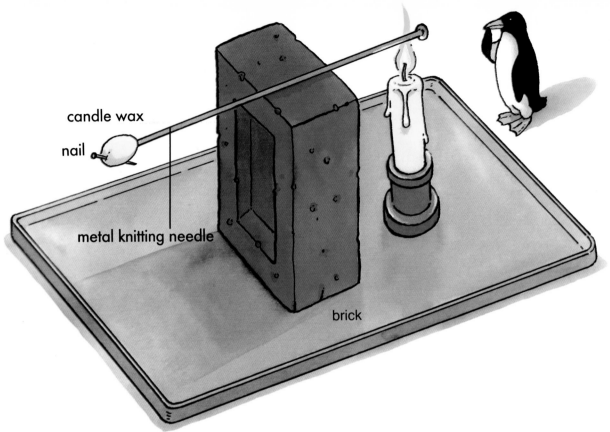

candle wax

nail

metal knitting needle

brick

Look at the picture. Think of what will happen to the candle wax and nail, now that the candle at the other end of the knitting needle has been lit.
The heat from the candle flame will pass quickly along the knitting needle and warm the wax so that it will begin to melt. The nail, no longer supported by the solid wax, will fall to the table.

glossary

Here are the meanings of some words you may have used for the first time in this book.

liquid: any substance that can flow, like water or oil.

lukewarm: fairly warm, neither hot nor cold.

material: any substance from which something can be made.

solid: a substance that keeps its shape, unlike a liquid or a gas.

temperature: the hotness or coldness of something.

thermometer: an instrument for measuring temperature.

weather: the conditions of sunshine, temperature, wind and rain at a particular time.

index